*This page intentionally left blank
because they made us.*

HOW TO STOP

Freaking

THE %#$@ OUT

(FOR THE WHOLE

FAM DAMNLY)

ERIN PASH AND KYLE KELLER

ILLUSTRATIONS BY KATIE HENRY

BEAVER'S POND PRESS
MINNEAPOLIS, MINNESOTA

Edited by Becca Hart and Hanna Kjeldbjerg
Proofread by Alicia Ester
Illustrated by Katie Henry
Production editor: Hanna Kjeldbjerg

ISBN 13: 978-1-64343-936-5
Library of Congress Catalog Number: 2019905020
Printed in the United States
First Printing: 2020
24 23 22 21 20   5 4 3 2 1

Book design and typesetting by Katie Henry.
Original design concept by Athena Currier.

Beaver's Pond Press
7108 Ohms Lane
Edina, MN 55439–2129
(952) 829-8818
www.BeaversPondPress.com

To order, visit www.ItascaBooks.com
or call (800) 901-3480 ext. 118. Reseller discounts available.

Contact Erin Pash and Kyle Keller at www.elliefamilyservices.com for school visits, speaking engagements, book club discussions, freelance writing projects, and interviews.

The authors wish to thank their parents for not totally screwing them up and for supporting their crazy, weird, and sometimes bizarre senses of humor (which they get from them) that has helped shape them as "stigma butt-kicking" mental health gurus working to make a difference in this world.

Disclaimer

The information in this book is meant to help people feel better by using several different types of self-regulation skills. If you find yourself experiencing a medical or mental health crisis, do NOT use this book in place of seeking prompt medical attention—call 911 or go to your local emergency room.

This book, while helpful to many, may also not help you. Hopefully if it doesn't, you are able to find some comedic relief. Then follow up with a professional for supportive services to address what could be an untreated medical or mental health issue.

The publisher, authors, and any other person who contributed to writing and publishing this book disclaim any liability from any injury or harm that may result from the use, proper or improper, of the information contained in this book. We are unable to guarantee that the information contained herein will, in fact, stop you from freaking out, and it should not be considered a substitute for your good judgment and common sense.

Lastly, nothing in this book should be construed or interpreted so as to infringe on the rights of other persons or to violate criminal statutes. Please be kind to others, property, and animals while using the information in this book.

If you REALLY want more information about our authors and their purpose, visit www.elliefamilyservices.com.

HAVE YOU EVER HEARD THE PHRASE
"MISERY LOVES COMPANY"?

You might think,

"WTF, why would I want someone else to suffer?"

Turns out, "misery loves company" is a real scientific thing . . .

but not in the way you might think.

HUMAN BEINGS PROCESS HARD %#$@ BETTER WHEN THEY DO IT WITH SOMEONE ELSE. All your brain really wants is for someone to say, "It's all good that you're freaking out."

When someone is patiently present with you, accepting your anxiety without dismissing or minimizing how you feel, it actually stops the freak-out in its track. It's magical (and neuroscience) but hey, the bottom line is you won't feel crappy anymore. It is really that simple.

THINK OF IT THIS WAY: Your brain freaking out is like a puppy needing attention. If you don't give the puppy attention it will keep bugging you for some love.

Sometimes this will be during dinner, or while you're trying to sleep, or when you're trying to do all the things. Sometimes it's really annoying so you try to just avoid the puppy. BUT! If you've ever had a puppy, you know the only way to stop a pup from needing attention is . . .

- BING BING BING -

You guessed it!

You gotta

GIVE IT ATTENTION!!

FEELINGS ARE THE SAME WAY. As soon as you give them attention, they stop annoying you. If we can find a buddy to talk to when we're losing our cool, it can help bring back our chill even faster, the same way giving a pup some intentional love will tucker the little guy out.

The next twenty-one skills are buddy-based activities (meant for two or more people) that can help you stop freaking out.

If you do them, you'll be a good doggie, oh yes you will be, what a good doggie you are.

Woof.

Burrito

STEP 1. Grab a human-sized blanket

STEP 2. Lay the blanket out on the floor

STEP 3. Lay on top of the blanket and hold on to its edge

STEP 4. Have your buddy roll you up

STEP 5. Become a human burrito

OPTIONAL:

Create one giant friendship burrito and talk about the best salsa you've ever had.

Catch

STEP 1. Grab something round

STEP 2. Throw it at your buddy

STEP 3. Cheer when your buddy catches it

STEP 4. Have your buddy throw it back to you

CAUTION:

Make sure your buddy is "engaged" in the game of catch . . . *before* you throw. Aim away from any vital organs.

Pick up Trash

STEP 1. Grab a bag (paper or plastic)

STEP 2. Go outside

STEP 3. Walk in any direction and pick up all the trash you see

STEP 4. Throw the trash away

STEP 5. Watch the litterbugs tremble

STEP 6. Wash hands (don't skip this step)

BONUS:

This buddy activity will also make you feel like a better human being . . . even though trash is gross #savetheplanet

Make Mac 'n' Cheese

STEP 1. Find a buddy who's hungry

STEP 2. Gather milk, noodles, butter, and cheese (if it's not in the house, bonus points for taking an outing to the store!)

STEP 3. Boil, drain, melt, mix

STEP 4. Nom!

OPTIONAL:

Make it fancy by adding Gouda or other pretentious cheese

Put on a Red Shirt

STEP 1. Find a red shirt

STEP 2. Put it on

STEP 3. Have your buddy snap a pic #powercolor

OPTIONAL:

Find a second red shirt for your
friend to put on #twinning

Look Through Photos

STEP 1. Look through photos

STEP 2. Find the best awkward photo

STEP 3. Share the wonderfully horrible pictures with a buddy

BONUS:

If you don't already have a mullet, find a guy or gal with a mullet and make it your profile pic. Mullets are just too good not to share with everyone.

Calming Yoga Pose

STEP 1. Go to Google

STEP 2. Type in "calming yoga pose"

STEP 3. Open "Images"

STEP 4. Pick five poses to do with your buddy

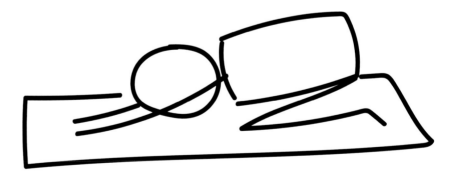

Puzzle a Puzzle

STEP 1. Find a puzzle

STEP 2. Do the outside edges first

STEP 3. Take a break

STEP 4. Maybe finish it, maybe not

Google "Baby Giraffe"

STEP 1. Go to Google

STEP 2. Type in "baby giraffe"

STEP 3. Open "Images"

STEP 4. *Awwwwwww*

STEP 5. Have your friend search for images of *their* favorite baby animal

STEP 6. Keep switching until you're not freaking out anymore

OPTIONAL:

Click through as many baby animals as you can!

Build a Tower

STEP 1. Find blocks, Legos, beer cans, etc.

STEP 2. See how high you can go

BONUS:

Destroy the tower!

Walk Around the Block

STEP 1. Find a friend

STEP 2. Go outside (shoes optional)

STEP 3. Start walking

STEP 4. Keep walking until you're not
freaking out anymore

OPTIONAL:

Count fire hydrants!
You'll be amazed at how
many there really are.

Complete the Animal Alphabet

STEP A. Act like an animal that starts with the letter *A*

STEP B. Have your friend act like an animal that starts with the letter *B*

STEP C. Keep switching

STEP Z. Get to *Z*

Become an Actor

STEP 1. Google "movie scene scripts"

STEP 2. Pick your characters. Rock-paper-scissors if necessary

STEP 3. Perform the lines like a Valley girl

SUGGESTIONS:

(From Beginner to Expert): *Legally Blonde*, *Clueless*, any Disney princess movie, *The Godfather*, *Batman*

MANDATORY:

If you can do the voice of the villain Bain from the Batman movies like a Valley girl, record and send to info@elliefamilyservices.com (not kidding)

Be a Dog

STEP 1. Bark

STEP 2. Sniff

STEP 3. Catch

STEP 4. Run

STEP 5. Sleep

CAUTION:

Do not greet your buddy like a dog. Not cool.

Plant a Seed

STEP 1. Find a seed with your buddy (apple, lemon, orange, tomato, etc.)

STEP 2. Plant it

STEP 3. Water it

STEP 4. Watch it grow and compare it with your buddy's plant

NOTE:

Doing this activity adds life to the world. Now how cool is that to think about? REAL. LIVING. LIFE!

Hold a Balancing Competition

STEP 1. Stand on one foot while your buddy does the same

STEP 2. Try and hold still for sixty seconds

STEP 3. Whoever does it longer w . . . wi. . . . will be freaking out less

Become a Songwriter

STEP 1. Pick anything. Literally anything.

STEP 2. Write a quick song about it

STEP 3. Sing your song to your buddy

STEP 4. Land major record deal

WARNING:

Impromptu songs can be very silly. Guffawing laughter may occur.

Wipe the Baseboards

STEP 1. Grab a warm damp cloth (one for every person!)

STEP 2. Pick a room

STEP 3. Clean the baseboards

STEP 4. See the dirt lift

STEP 5. Feel your mood lift

OPTIONAL:

Listen to the song *So Fresh, So Clean* by OutKast. There will be nobody as dope as you, you're just so fresh and so clean, clean.

Make a Snow Angel

STEP 1. Find an open space on the floor or outside

STEP 2. Do the snow angel motion

STEP 3. Count "one-Mississippi, two-Mississippi," all the way up to sixty

STEP 4. Have your buddy record you in "loop" or "boomerang" mode

Play Chess

STEP 1. Play it

STEP 2. If you don't know how, learn with your buddy

STEP 3. If learning a new board game feels frustrating, be frustrated with your buddy

STEP 4. Chess is hard

See a Therapist

STEP 1. Research a therapist (try psychologytoday.com)

STEP 2. Pick up the phone

STEP 3. Make the call

STEP 4. Tell your friends

LET'S TALK A LITTLE ABOUT THERAPY . . .

Therapy is helpful for every person who's ever existed. One of the authors' goals is to help people realize that going to therapy is the NORMAL way to treat brains and feelings. It sure beats the alternative of keeping it all in, feeling bummed out, or worse, taking on eating paint chips as a new hobby (really, this is very bad).

Having difficulty coping with feelings is a NORMAL part of human existence. Research shows that 1 in 4 people have depression, 50 percent of the population has anxiety, and 100 percent of all people have experienced complicated or conflicting feelings at some point in their lives. We're not great at math but we're feeling pretty confident that 100 percent is the same as everyone.

It's also NORMAL to have mixed feelings about saying this stuff out loud. Our answer to this? It's awkward for us too. So let's be awkward together and have fun while talking about all the feels.

About the Authors

ERIN PASH is a marriage and family therapist who lives in the suburbs of the Twin Cities. She is the co-owner of Ellie Family Services, and her life's mission is to make getting help more fun, accessible, and creative. Erin does the whole mom thing when she's not working and has a flair for human anatomy, art, and golf.

Erin's favorite buddy skill is definitely the burrito. She "makes" her kids do it to her until they are all laughing so hard they pee in their pants (change of clothes optional).

KYLE KELLER is a licensed clinical social worker and has spent his entire life living on the outskirts of St. Paul, Minnesota. He is the co-owner of Ellie Family Services and seeks to help connect others to their personal sources of meaning and value, and facilitate conversations that normalize and destigmatize various forms of distress. Kyle is a big fan of reading, music, and world history.

Kyle's favorite buddy skill is making up songs with his brother. They will literally make up and sing songs about anything and everything including (but not limited to) buttered toast, porcupines, things that look like butt cracks, and of course, miniature horses.

About Ellie Family Services

ELLIE FAMILY SERVICES opened in 2015 with the mission to offer creativity in the delivery of family wellness services. After years of working in nonprofits and government, co-founders Erin and Kyle realized that they could fill gaps in the mental health field and challenge mental health stigma by implementing their unique framework for treating the whole family.

Ellie Family Services has four clinic locations in St. Paul, Woodbury, Lakeville, and Minneapolis, Minnesota, and serves over 3,500 families in these communities. Taking the humor approach, incorporating new ideas, and hiring staff with passion for the mission, Ellie Family Services continues to grow by the day. The Ellie team is excited to better the lives of everyday families through the creation and delivery of innovative and customized wellness programs, goods, and services—like this book!

elliefamilyservices.com